Thinking about the Seasons

Summer

Clare Collinson

SEA-TO-SEA

Mankato Collingwood London

This edition first published in 2011 by
Sea-to-Sea Publications
Distributed by Black Rabbit Books
P.O. Box 3263, Mankato, Minnesota 56002

Printed in China, Dongguan

Library of Congress Cataloging-in-Publication Data

Collinson, Clare.
  Summer / Clare Collinson.
      p. cm. -- (Thinking about the seasons)
  Includes index.
  ISBN 978-1-59771-261-3 (library bound)
 1. Summer--Juvenile literature. I. Title.
  QB637.6.C65 2011
  508.2--dc22

                                        2009052821

9 8 7 6 5 4 3 2

Published by arrangement with the Watts Publishing Group Ltd, London.

Planning and production by Discovery Books Limited
Managing editor: Laura Durman
Editor: Clare Collinson
Picture researcher: Rachel Tisdale
Designer: Ian Winton

Photographs: Chris Fairclough: p. 4, 9; Getty Images: title page (Kane Skennar), p. 8 (P. Broze & A. Chederros),
p. 10 (Ariel Skelley), p. 11 (Leon Giran-Max/Fine Art Photographic), p. 18 (Imagno), p. 20 (Michelle Quance), p. 22
(Larry Dale Gordon), p. 23 (Image Source), p. 24 (Flying Colours Ltd), p. 26 (Gregory Costanzo), p. 28 (Bigshots),
p. 29 (Brian Summers), p. 30 (English School); istockphoto.com: p. 5 (Tinas Bercic), p. 6 (Nathan Gleave), p. 7 (Chan
Pak Kei), p. 12 (Adam Tinney), p. 14 (Jello5700), p. 16 (Can Balcioglu), p. 17 (Ali-Lan Lee), p. 19 (Tony Svensson),
p. 21 (Joselito Briones), p. 25 (Chutima Chokkij), p. 31 (Josef Philipp); Shutterstock Images: p. 15 (Jean Frooms)

Cover photos: istockphoto.com: Jacek Chabraszewski, Jakub Semeniuk.

Page 11 *Woman in a Poppy Field* (c.1900), Leon Giran-Max
Page 18 *Wheatfield and Cypress Trees* (1889), Vincent Van Gogh
Page 30 *The Fair* (20th century), English School
"Sand" by John Foster (1991) from *Four O'Clock Friday* (Oxford University Press) is included by
permission of the author. Every attempt has been made to clear copyright. Should there be any inadvertent omission
please apply to the Publishers for rectification.

March 2010
RD/6000006414/002

Contents

When I think of summer, I think of fun! Summer is a good time to play outside.

Summer is one of the four seasons of the year—spring, summer, fall, and winter. Summer is the warmest season.

In summer, the sun is strong and high in the sky. The sun rises early in summer and sets late, so the days are long.

Many flowers bloom in the summer sun.

What kinds of flowers make you think of summer?

I like warm days in summer when the sky is clear blue. Sometimes there are fluffy white clouds. Gentle breezes help keep you cool.

On some days in summer, the weather is humid. The air feels damp and sticky, and there is no wind.

How do you stay cool on hot summer days?

Sometimes in summer there are storms. The clouds are dark, and heavy rain may fall. Have you heard the rumble of thunder in summer?

Why should you stay inside in a thunderstorm?

In summer, I wear light clothes. When it is really hot, I wear a T-shirt and shorts, and sandals or flip-flops on my feet. A hat helps me keep cool.

What summer clothes do you wear?

The sun's rays are strong in summer.
I use sunscreen to stop my skin from
burning and don't stay out in the
sun for too long.

In summer, gardens are full of bright-colored flowers. Plants grow quickly in summer.

If the weather is dry, plants can become thirsty. You may need to water them.

This painting makes me think of fields full of poppies in summer.

Where have you seen wildflowers in summertime?

Trees are covered in green leaves in
summer. On hot days, I like to relax
in the shade of a big tree.

The Beech Tree

I'd like to have a garden
With a beech tree on the lawn;
The little birds that lived there
Would wake me up at dawn.

And in the summer weather
When all the leaves were green,
I'd sit beneath the beech boughs
And see the sky between.

Rose Fyleman

In summer, birds come into my garden to feed on insects and worms. They help gardeners by eating snails and caterpillars, too.

Have you seen birds splashing in water on hot days?

Young frogs and toads come out of the water in summer. Birds and foxes like to eat frogs and toads.

How do you think frogs and toads hide from birds and foxes?

In summer, the air buzzes with the sound of wasps and bees, and I often see butterflies fluttering by.

What other insects have you seen in summer?

Butterflies lay eggs,
which hatch into caterpillars.
Caterpillars love to munch on leaves.

The Caterpillar

Brown and furry
Caterpillar in a hurry
Take your walk
To the shady leaf or stalk.
May no toad spy you,
May the little birds pass by you,
Spin and die,
To live again a butterfly.

Christina Rossetti

Do you know how a caterpillar becomes a butterfly?

This painting makes me think of fields full of golden wheat. Warm sunshine makes wheat grow really tall.

Have you seen wheat swaying in the summer breeze?

Some crops, such as wheat, corn, and oats, become ripe in summer. In late summer, when the crops are fully grown, farmers start to harvest them.

Many kinds of fruit are ready to pick in summer. I love the taste of juicy ripe strawberries.

Which is your favorite summer fruit?

In spring, fruit trees have flowers called blossoms. In summer, the blossoms become young fruit.

Have you seen small apples growing on trees in summer? The apples will be ready to pick in fall.

What other kinds of fruits grow on trees?

In the summer sunshine, it's fun to eat outside. We sometimes have barbecues or go to the park for a picnic. I eat lots of corn on the cob and salad—yummy!

What kind of food do you like to eat outside in summer?

What is your
favorite flavor
of ice cream?

When it's very hot, I really like eating
ice cream. I drink lots of water in
summer, too. It helps me keep cool.

When schools close for the summer, many people go away on vacation.

Roads can become very busy because lots of cars leave cities and towns.

When I go on vacation, I send postcards to my friends.

Tuesday

Dear Emily,
We are staying in a hotel near the beach. It is very sunny here and the sea is really warm. Today we are going for a ride on a boat!
Love from Alisha xxx

Emily Wells

17 Sandfield Dr.

Boston, MA

02114

In summer, I like to play on the beach.
I build sand castles and search for seashells.
I jump in waves as they splash against the
shore.

What do you like doing on the beach?

Sand

Sand in your fingernails
Sand between your toes
Sand in your earholes
Sand up your nose!

Sand in your sandwiches
Sand on your bananas
Sand in your bed at night
Sand in your pajamas!

Sand in your sandals
Sand in your hair
Sand in your panties
Sand everywhere!

John Foster

At school in summer, we play tennis and other outdoor sports. At the end of the year, we have a sports day.

Does your school have a sports day in summer?

The days are long in summer, so I often play outside in the evening. I play football and baseball and I ride my bike.

What games and sports do you like playing in summer?

This painting makes me think of summer fairs.

Does the fair ever come to your local town?

In summer, I like to go to carnivals. It's fun to hear the music and watch the dancers. There are lots of special costumes to see.

What do you like doing in the summertime? Are there other things that make you think of summer?

Index